# How to play
# DRUMS

## by
## Peter Gelling

**Published by**
**KOALA MUSIC PUBLICATIONS**

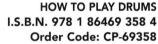

**HOW TO PLAY DRUMS**
**I.S.B.N. 978 1 86469 358 4**
**Order Code: CP-69358**
**Acknowledgments**
Cover Photograph: Phil Martin
Photographs: Phil Martin

For more information on this series contact;
Koala Music Publications
email: info@koalamusicpublications.com
or visit our website;
**www.koalamusicpublications.com**

# Contents

# Introduction

**How To Play Drums** assumes that you have little or no prior knowledge of music or playing the drums. Starting from learning the parts of the drumkit, how to sit at the drums and how to hold the drum sticks, you are introduced to:

1. Reading and understanding music as it relates to the drums.
2. Learning to play using all the drums and cymbals which make up the drum kit and gaining control of all four limbs.
3. Playing drum beats in a variety of styles including Rock, Blues Funk and Jazz.
4. How to invent your own drum beats and fills.
5. How to make your drum parts work with other instruments, in particular the bass and guitar.

**All drummers should know all of the information contained in this book.**
After completing this book you will have a solid basic understanding of the drums and will be ready to move on to more advanced study of specific musical styles.

The best and fastest way to learn is to use this book in conjunction with:
1. Practicing and playing with other musicians. It is surprising how good a basic drums/bass/guitar combination can sound, even when playing easy music;

2. In the early stages it is helpful to have the guidance of an experienced teacher. This will help you maintain a steady practice schedule and obtain weekly goals.

# Using the Recording

This book comes with an accompanying CD and DVD. The book shows you which drums to play and what technique to use and the recording lets you hear how each example should sound. Practice the examples slowly at first, gradually increasing tempo. Once you are confident you can play the example evenly without losing the beat, try playing along with the recording. You will hear a hi-hat beat at the beginning of each example, to lead you into the example and to help you keep time. A small diagram of a compact disc with a number as shown below indicates a recorded example. Some of the tracks on the CD contain more than one example. In these cases, index points have been used (1.0, 1.1, 1.2 etc). If your CD player has an index points function, you can select each example individually. If not, each example will automatically follow the previous one.

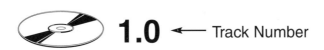 **1.0** ← Track Number

# Lesson 1

## Understanding the Drum Kit

Before you begin playing the drums, it is important to know what the different parts of the drumkit are called. The photo below shows a common basic setup. The kit shown here contains three tom toms, but many drummers use only two as these are probably the least necessary part of the kit. In fact, most drum parts can be played using only the snare drum, the bass drum and the hi hat cymbals, so don't worry if you have a very basic setup. The **bass drum** is played with the right foot and produces what is often called the "bottom end" sound of the drums. The **snare drum** is usually played with the left hand, but the right hand is also used for certain beats as well as playing fills. The **hi hat and ride cymbals** are generally played with the right hand, but once again the left hand may be used in certain situations. The **crash cymbal** may be played with either hand, depending on which one is most practical for each musical situation. The **tom toms** (toms for short) can also be played by either hand. **The hi hat cymbals can also be played by the left foot** and certain sounds using the open hi hats are achieved by using a combination of the right hand and the left foot. As you can see, becoming a good drummer requires the use of all four limbs. Through the course of this book you will be introduced to all of the sounds mentioned here and by the end you should be confident playing in a band in most styles of music.

# Sitting Position

The most important aspect of sitting at the drums is to keep your back straight. This gives you maximum reach and avoids the possibility of muscle strains. Start by sitting with the snare drum directly in front of you. The exact distance is a personal choice, experiment until you feel comfortable with the position of both the drum stool and the snare drum.

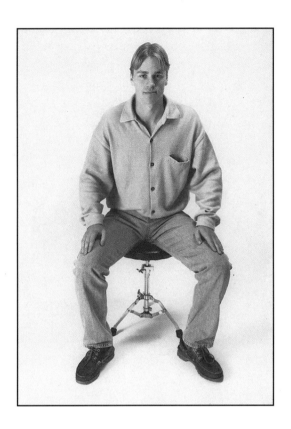

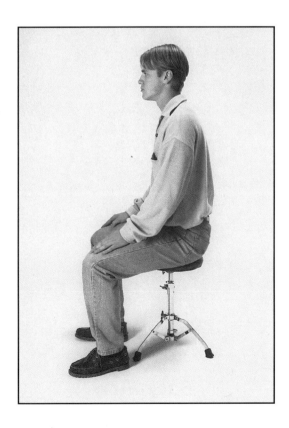
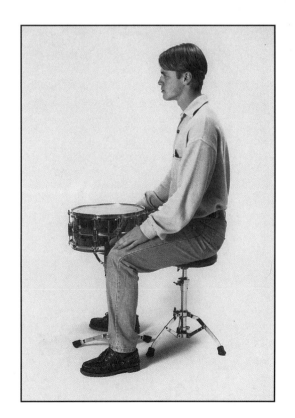

When setting up the position of the drum stool and the kit, make sure you can reach all the drums and cymbals easily without having to lean or stretch. Also make sure that everything is far apart enough that your arm movement is not restricted. The most important thing is to be in a relaxed and comfortable position when you are playing.

**Front View**

**Side View**

**Top View**

**Back View**

# Drum Stick Grip

There are two basic ways of holding the drum sticks, one is called **traditional grip** and the other is **match grip**. In traditional grip, each hand holds the stick differently. This grip evolved out of marching band snare drum playing where the snare drum is held to one side. However, this method has no practical advantage when applied to the modern drumkit. For beginning drummers it is more practical to use **match grip** which means that both hands hold the sticks the same way in the manner shown in the photos below.

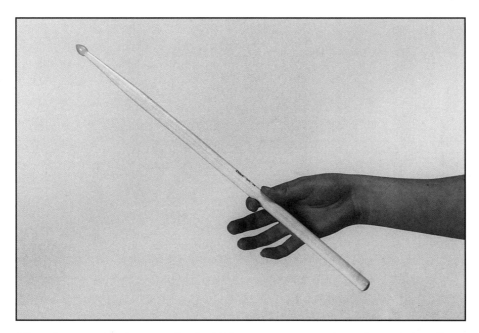

The drum stick is usually held between your **thumb** and the **first** joint of your **index finger**.

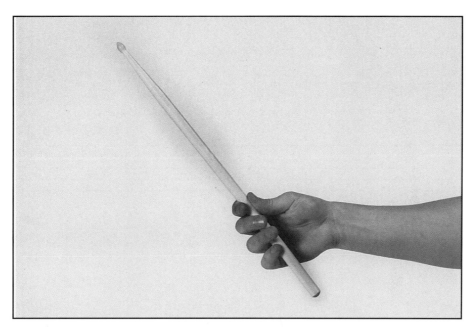

Close the other fingers loosely around the drum stick. Don't grip the stick with these fingers. They are merely a support to the stick rather than part of the grip itself.

# How to Read Music

Drum music is commonly written on the **Stave** or **Staff**. This is made up of **five** lines and **four** spaces.

**Stave or Staff**

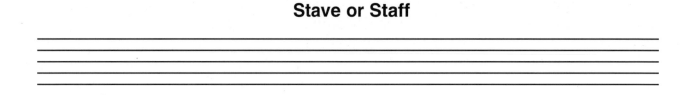

The Staff is divided into sections with **Bar Lines**.

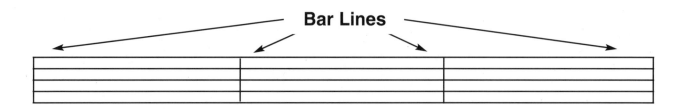

Each section between the Bar lines is called **one bar or one measure**.

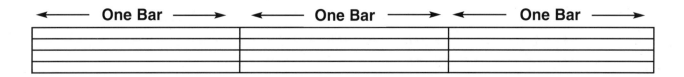

**A Double Bar** line indicates the end of the music, or the end of a section such as a verse or chorus.

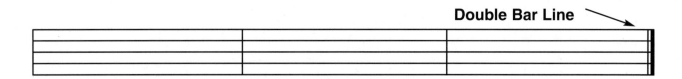

**Two Dots** next to a double bar line are called a **repeat sign** and indicate that the music is to be repeated from the beginning, or from a previous repeat sign.

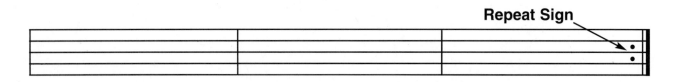

Here is another sign called a **Bar Repeat Sign** which indicates that the previous bar is to be repeated. If the same bar is to be played several times in succession, repeat signs are often used.

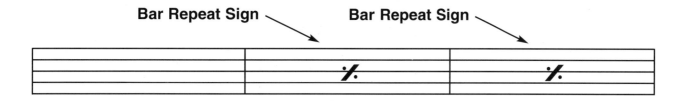

The bass clef sign is used at the beginning of each line of drum music.

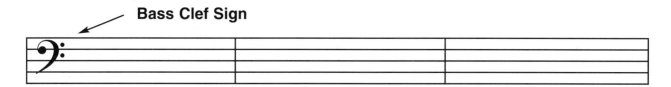

The **Time Signature** appears next to the Bass Clef Sign and indicates how many beats are to be played in each bar and what type of notes these beats represent. The time signature shown here is the **four four** time signature which indicates four quarter note beats per bar.

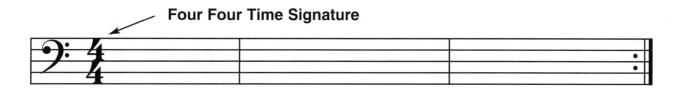

Drum music is usually written in the spaces of the staff, including the space above the staff, to represent different parts of the drum kit. The most commonly used system is shown below.

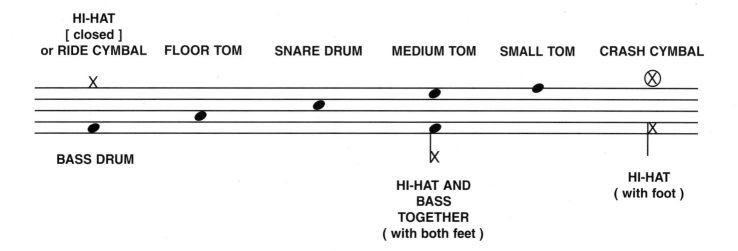

# Lesson 2

## Note and Rest Values

The longest note commonly used in music is the whole note, which lasts four beats. The table below shows how the whole note can be divided into shorter notes. Whole notes and half notes are not common in drum notation but are very common in music written for other instruments and are definitely worth learning to recognise and count.

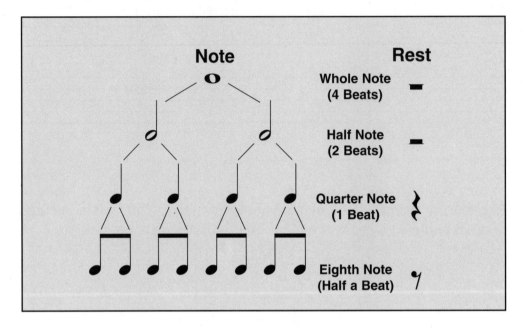

## Notes Used in Drum Beats

The note values most commonly used in drum notation are the quarter note, the eighth note and the sixteenth note. Most drum beats and patterns are made up of combinations of some or all of these note types.

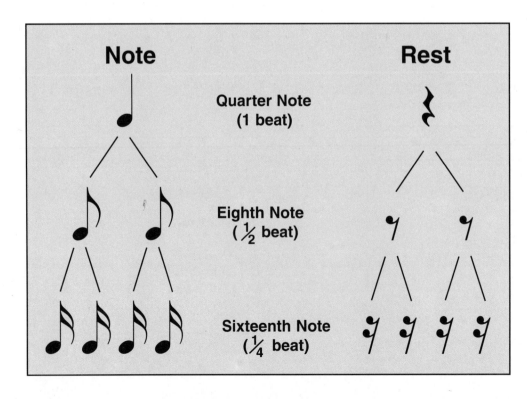

## The Whole Note

This is a **whole note**.
It lasts for **four** beats.
There is **one** whole note in one bar of $\frac{4}{4}$ time.

Count: **1** 2 3 4

## The Whole Rest

This symbol is a **whole rest.** It indicates **four beats** of silence. **Small** counting numbers are placed under rests.

Count: 1 2 3 4

The following example contains eight bars of music to be played on the snare drum. It uses only whole notes and whole rests. It is important to count out loud as you play and keep a steady tempo. Play the example with the right hand and then the left hand, then try alternating.

 **1.0**

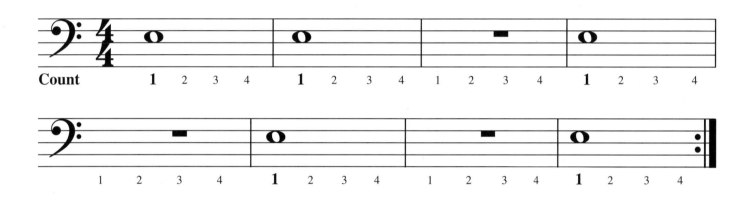

## The Half Note

This music note is called a **half note**. It has a value of **two** beats. There are **two** half notes in one bar of $\frac{4}{4}$ time.

Count: **1** 2

## The Half Rest

This symbol is a **half rest.** It indicates **two beats** of silence.

Count: 1 2

 **1.1**

This example makes use of the half note and the half rest. Once again, be sure to count out loud as you play and practice it with both the right and left hands.

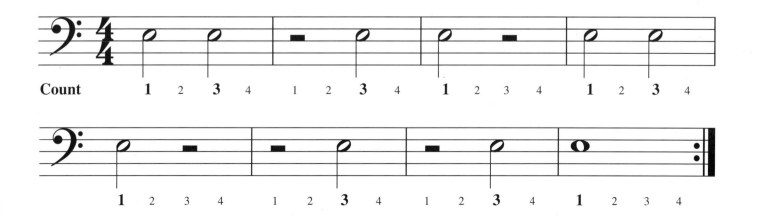

12

## The Quarter Note

This is a **quarter note**. It lasts for one beat.
There are four quarter notes in one bar of $\frac{4}{4}$ time.

Count: 1

## The Quarter Rest

This symbol is a **quarter rest**. It indicates **one beat** of silence.

Count: 1

 1.2

The following example uses quarter notes and quarter rests. There are several ways to play this example. First, alternate the hands **RLRL** and then reverse them (**LRLR**). Once you can do this strongly and evenly at a reasonable tempo, play the example with one hand at a time (**RRRR** etc and **LLLL** etc). This will help to prepare you for actual drum beats and fills.

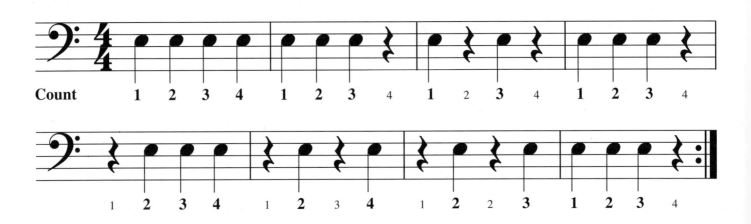

 1.3

This example uses whole notes, half notes and quarter notes. Remember to keep an even tempo and count out loud as you play. Counting is very important for drummers, as the rest of the band will be relying on you to keep solid time even if they make mistakes! Counting out loud right from the beginning, along with the use of a metronome or drum machine is the best way to develop a good sense of time.

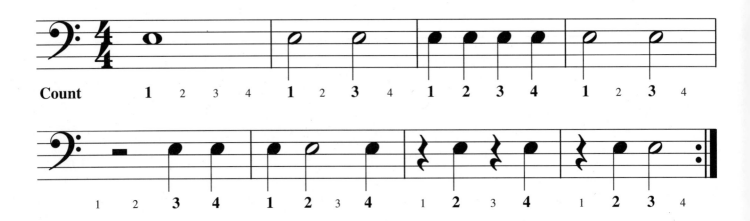

# Building a Drum Beat

Most drum beats require the use of three limbs and sometimes all four. When learning any new beat, it is a good idea to practice coordinating two limbs at a time before combining all the parts. In the following example, the bass drum is played with the right foot on every beat and the snare drum is played with the left hand.

**2.0**

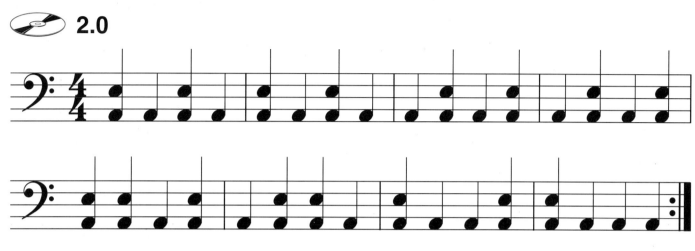

**2.1**

In this example, the right hand plays either the hi hat or ride cymbal (try one and then the other) on every beat and the bass drum is varied.

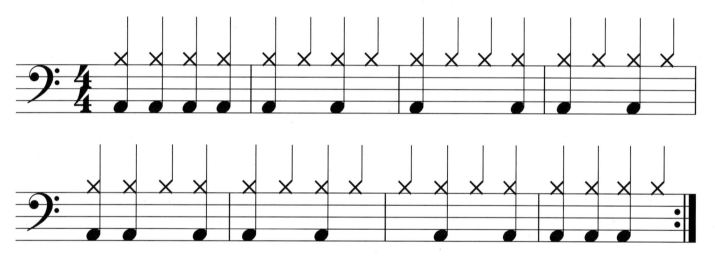

**2.2**

Once again the right hand plays the cymbal, but this time it is played in conjunction with the snare drum.

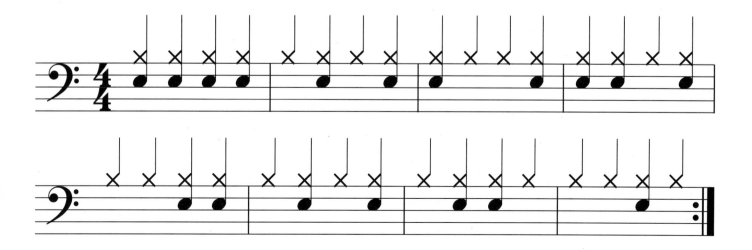

 **3.0**

This example is a full drum beat based on quarter notes. The right hand plays quarter notes on every beat, the left hand plays on the 2nd and 4th beats and the right foot plays on the 1st and 3rd beats. The alternation between bass drum and snare drum is a common element drumming in many styles of music. The use of the snare drum on beats 2 and 4 is called a **backbeat**.

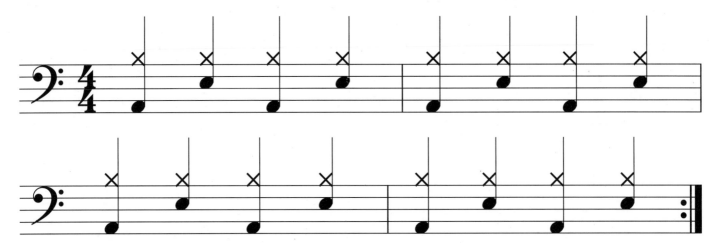

Here are a couple of variations on this basic beat. In the following example, the bass drum is used on every beat.

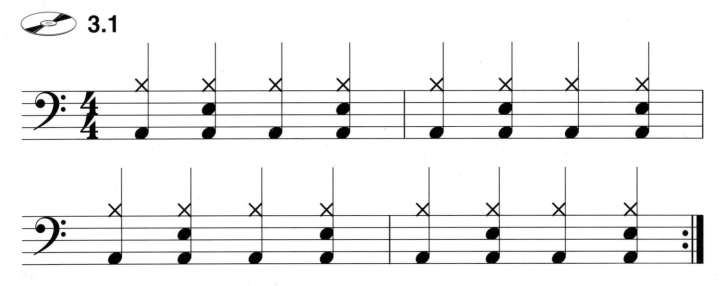 **3.1**

 **3.2**

This one is a combination of the previous two beats. The bass drum is used on all four beats in the last bar. This helps build momentum for a return to the beginning.

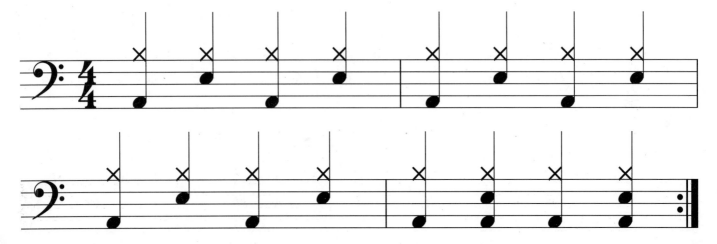

# Lesson 3

## The Eighth Note

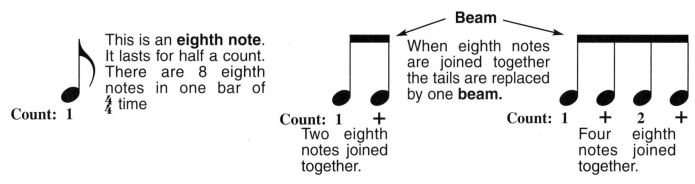

The following example shows a constant stream of eighth notes played on the snare drum. Alternate the hands **RLRL** and then reverse them (**LRLR**). Once you can do this strongly and **evenly** at a reasonable tempo, play the example with one hand at a time (**RRRR** etc and **LLLL** etc). Once again, remember to count out loud as you play.

### 4.0

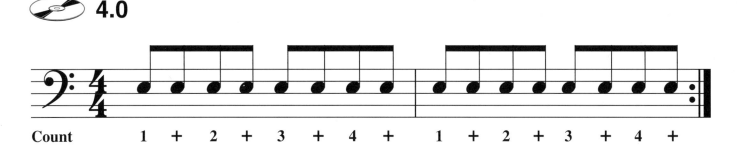

The next important step in gaining control of eighth notes is to play them on the hi hat and ride cymbal with the right hand as demonstrated in the following example. It is important to keep the notes even and the sound consistent.

### 4.1

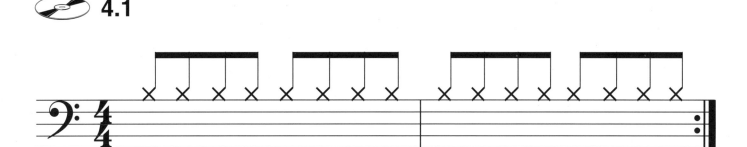

### 4.2

Once you are comfortable playing eighth notes with the right hand, try adding the backbeat on the snare drum with the left hand.

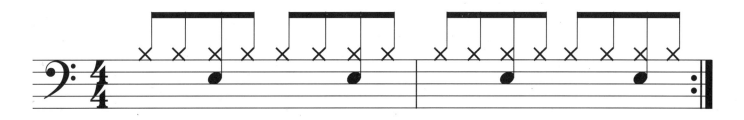

The following example uses the bass drum in conjunction with the constant eighth notes played by the right hand.

 **4.3**

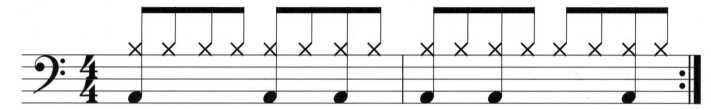

# Rock Beats

Once you are comfortable playing the previous examples, you are ready to play a basic Rock beat. The following examples demonstrate two simple rock beats. The only difference between these beats is the placement of the bass drum. In the first one, the bass drum is played on beats 1 and 3 only, while the second one has the bass drum on all four beats. Practice each one slowly at first and then once you are comfortable with them, try playing along with the recording. Once you can play these beats, you are ready to start playing with other musicians. At the beginning of example 6, you will see a **C** symbol after the bass clef sign. This represents **common time**, which means exactly the same as $\frac{4}{4}$

**5.**

**6.**

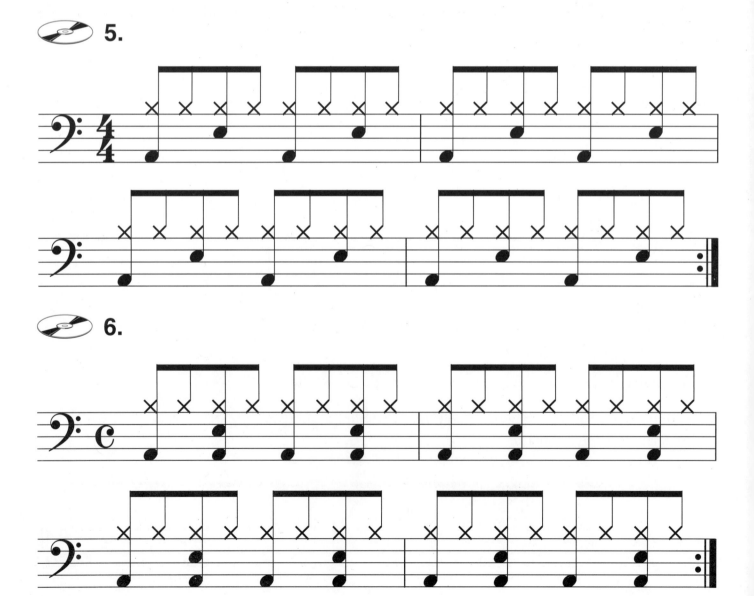

# The Eighth Rest

This symbol is a **eighth rest.** It indicates **half a beat** of silence.

Here is a note reading exercise which makes use of the eighth rest. When using rests, counting is particularly important so you don't get lost and play notes in the wrong place.

**7.**

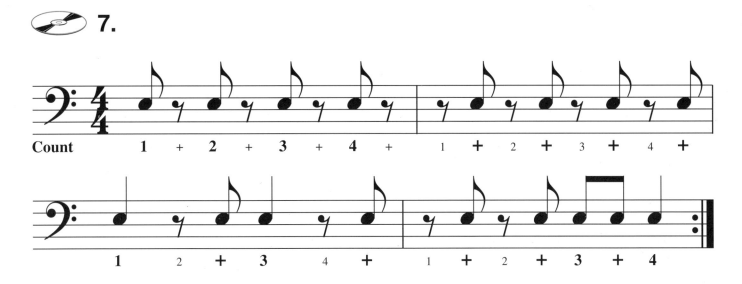

# Snare Drum Control

To play the drums well, you need to be able to place any kind of note on or in between any beat with any limb independently from the parts played by the other limbs. A good way to start developing this ability is to play a basic beat and then vary one of the parts. The following examples should help you become confident with varying your snare drum parts. First try example 8 which uses only the right and left hands.

**8**

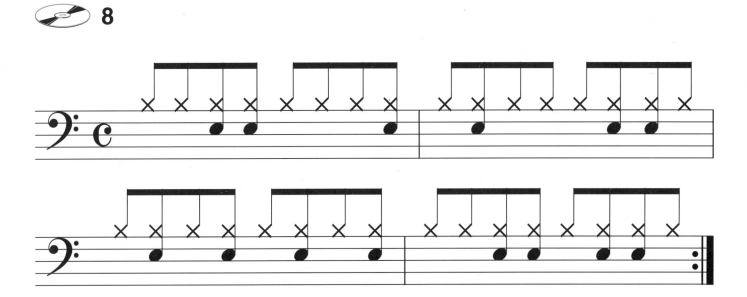

Now try the following examples which make use of the right and left hands along with the right foot. When you are comfortable with these, try making up some variations of your own.

 **9.**

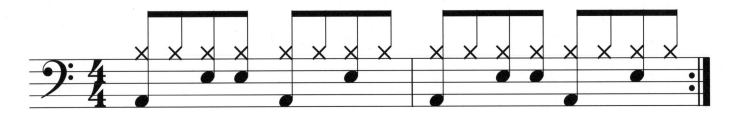

 **10.**

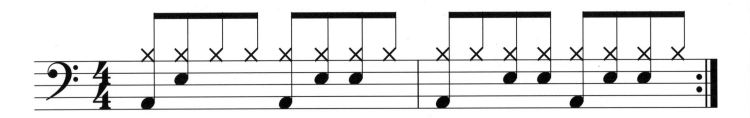

 **11.**

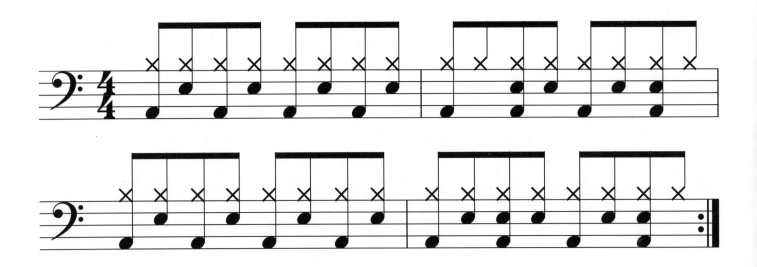

# Bass Drum Control

As well as the snare drum, it is common to play the bass drum in many different parts of the bar. Here are some examples to help you gain control of using eighth notes on the bass drum. Once again, be sure to count as you play and play all the notes with a consistent volume and tone.

 **12.0**

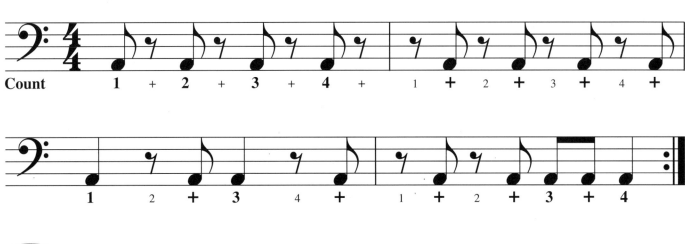

 **12.1**

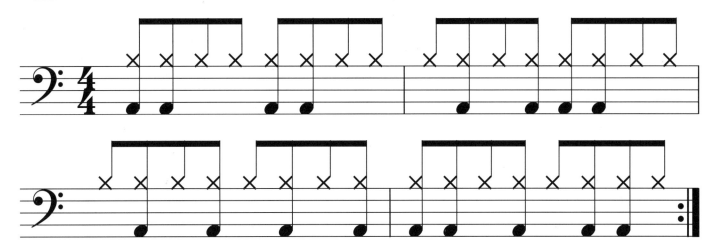

 **13.**

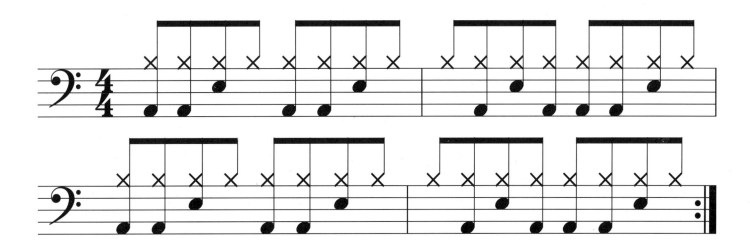

The following examples demonstrate several commonly used bass drum patterns. These beats are used in a variety of styles of music including Rock, R&B, Hip-Hop, Soul, Country and Heavy Metal.

**14.**

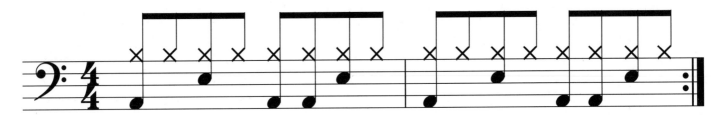

**15.**

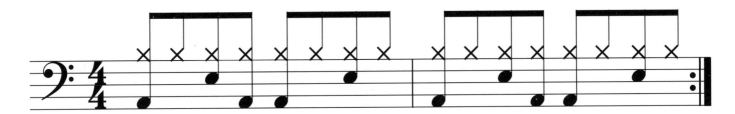

**16.**

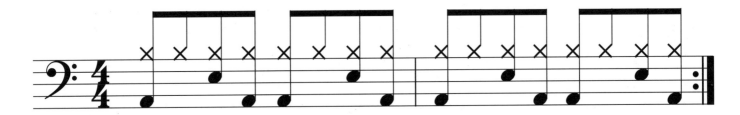

**17.**

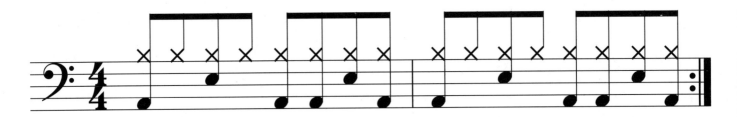

**18.**

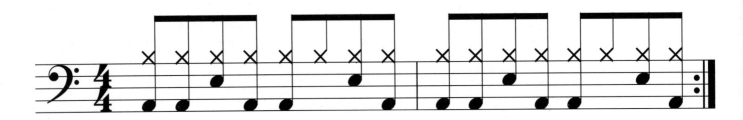

# Lesson 4

## Playing Fills

Once you can play a variety of basic beats, you are ready to start playing fills. A **fill** (or fill-in) is a musical idea that breaks away from the basic beat and leads into either a new section or a repeat of the basic beat. The easiest way to start playing fills is to leave your basic pattern and play a bar of eighth notes on the snare drum before returning to the basic beat, as demonstrated in the following example. When playing the snare drum fill in bar 2, begin with the right hand and then alternate both hands. Take care not to speed up or slow when changing between the fill and the beat.

 **19.**

 **20.**

Now try this variation. The fill here is played on the snare drum and the small and medium tom toms. Once again the fill is played with alternate sticking, beginning with the right hand. When learning to play fills, it is useful to keep the bass drum going on each beat as demonstrated here.

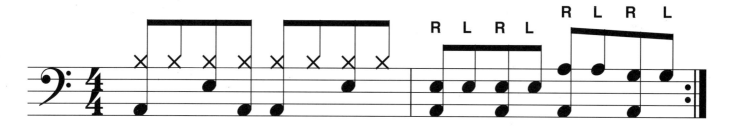

 **21.0**

Here are some examples using which should help you get comfortable moving around the drum kit. This first one alternates between the snare drum and the small and medium tom toms.

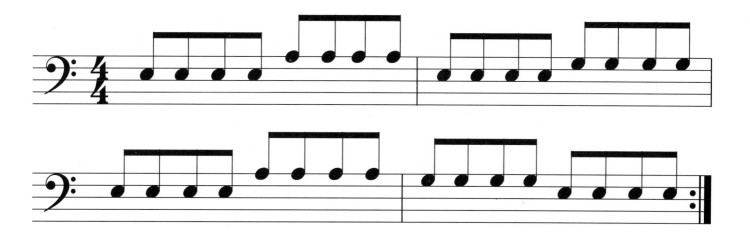

 **21.1**

This example moves around between all three tom toms and the snare drum.

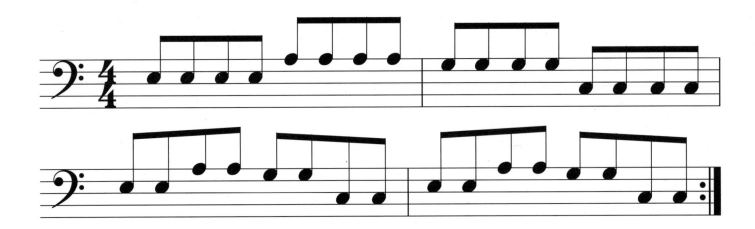

 **22.**

Once you are comfortable moving around the drums, try alternating a fill with a basic beat as shown in this example.

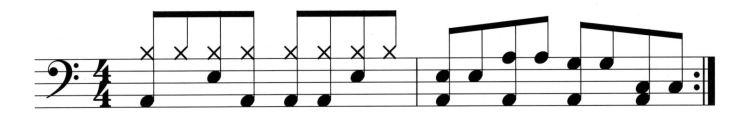

# Using the Crash Cymbal

Another part of the drumkit you will need to become familiar with is the **crash cymbal**. It can be played with either hand, but for now, use the right hand. In the following example, the right hand moves between the crash cymbal and the hi hat. Play slowly at first and remember to count.

 **23.**

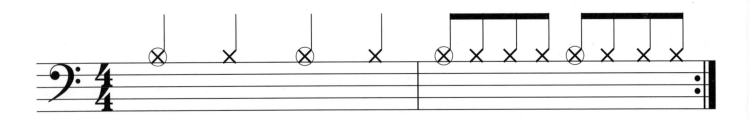

In this example, the crash cymbal is played along with the basic beat. This can be useful when you want to add some extra drama to a certain part of a song, e.g. during a lead guitar solo.

 **24.0**

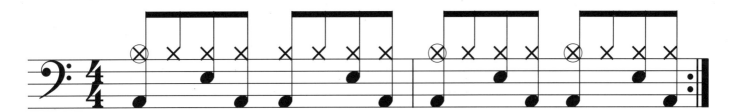

One of the most common places the crash cymbal is used is directly after a fill has been played. The fill often finishes with the left hand and the right hand plays the crash on the first beat of the following bar before settling back into the basic beat. Listen to the following example on the CD to hear how effectively this works.

 **24.1**

# 12 Bar Blues

**12 Bar Blues** is a form of music containing a **chord progression** which repeats every 12 bars. A chord is a group of notes played together by an instrument like a guitar or keyboard. A chord progression is a group of chords played in succession before repeating. Chords will be discussed in lesson 10. There are hundreds of well known songs based on the 12 bar Blues progression, i.e., they contain basically the same chords in the same order. 12 bar Blues is one of the most common progressions in Blues, Jazz and Rock. Every drummer will be asked to play a 12 bar Blues at some stage. In fact it is very likely to be one of the first progressions used at a jam session. When playing a 12 bar Blues, try playing a fill at the end of every four bars. This will correspond with some of the chord changes played by the other instruments and will help build momentum in the song. Listen to the recording of the following example to hear how effective this sounds.

Some well known songs which use this 12 bar chord pattern are:

Original Batman T.V. Theme
Hound Dog - Elvis Presley
Johnny B. Goode - Chuck Berry
Blue Suede Shoes - Elvis Presley
Killing Floor - Jimi Hendrix
Sweet Home Chicago - Blues Brothers

Pride and Joy - Stevie Ray Vaughan
Ice Cream Man - Van Halen
Surfin' U.S.A. - The Beach Boys
Good Golly Miss Molly - Little Richard
Oh Pretty Woman - Gary Moore

**25. 12 Bar Blues**

Notice the fills in this example. Each one is slightly different, which keeps the sound interesting. The fill in bar 8 lasts only two beats. This is just as common as a full bar fill. Experiment with other beats and fills on the 12 bar Blues form. If you are playing in a band, listen to what the other players are doing and try to make your part fit in with theirs. Don't be afraid to try variations and use the crash cymbal where you think it sounds good.

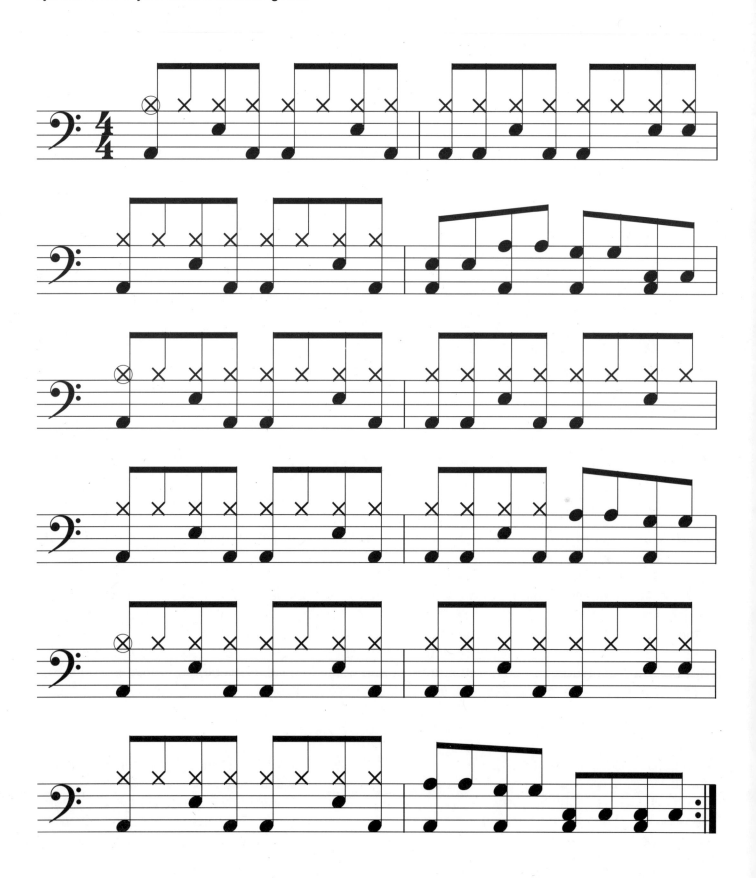

# Lesson 5

## The Triplet

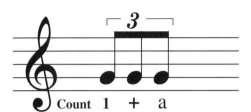

An eighth note **triplet** is a group of **three** evenly spaced notes played within one beat. Eighth note triplets are indicated by three eighth notes grouped together by a bracket (or a curved line) and the numeral *3*. The eighth note triplets are played with one third of a beat each. Triplets are easy to understand once you have heard them played. Listen to example 26.0 on the CD to hear the effect of triplets.

 ### 26.0 How to Count Triplets

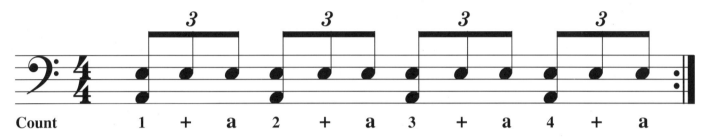

Once you are confident counting triplets, try alternating between a bar of eighth notes and a bar of eighth note triplets as shown in the following example. It is best to do this exercise with a drum machine or metronome to make sure you don't speed up or slow down as you change between the two rhythms.

 ### 26.1

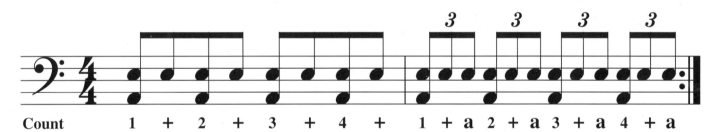

Now try this beat which uses triplets played by the right hand. Once again, remember to keep the notes even and the sound consistent.

 ### 27

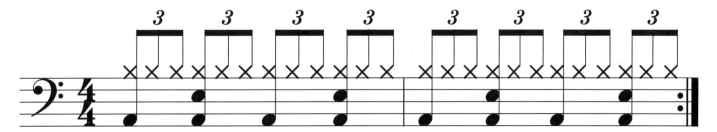

# Bass and Snare Drum Variations

As with any new rhythm or beat subdivision, it is important to practice playing triplets on any beat on the snare drum and the bass drum. Here are some examples to help you gain control of triplets on the bass drum.

 **28.**

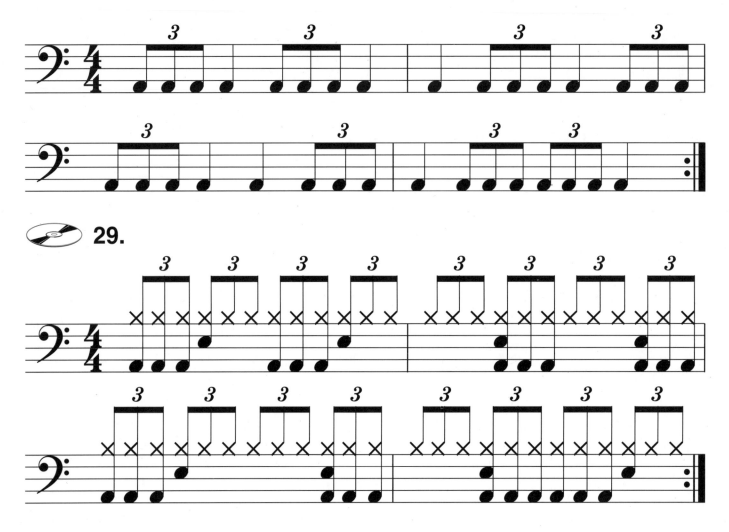

**29.**

**30.**

Now try this example which features triplets on the snare drum. Keep all the parts strong and steady regardless of what the left hand is doing.

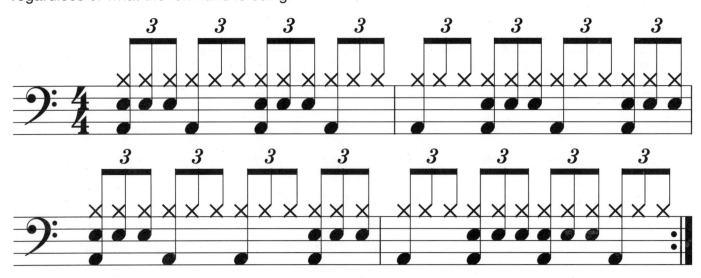

 **31.**

Here is a commonly used Blues beat which uses triplets. Notice the triplet figure on the bass drum and also on the snare drum just before the crash cymbal is played.

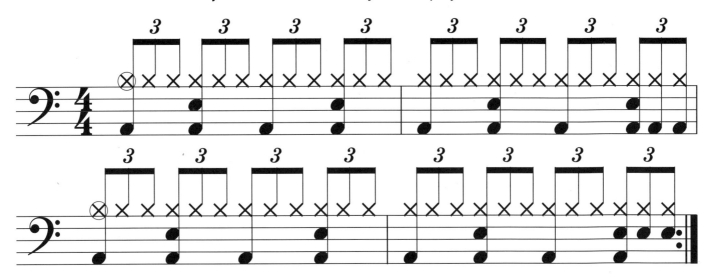

# Fills Using Triplets

 **32.**

When playing fills using triplets, each new beat starts with the opposite hand to the previous beat. Try playing the following example **RLR LRL** etc, and then **LRL RLR** etc. Another useful technique is to play all the notes on a particular drum with one hand, e.g. **RRR LLL** etc.

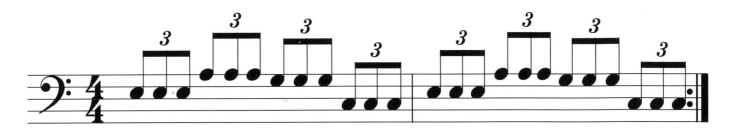

 **33.**

Once you are comfortable moving around the drums using triplets, try alternating between a basic triplet beat and a one bar fill as demonstrated here.

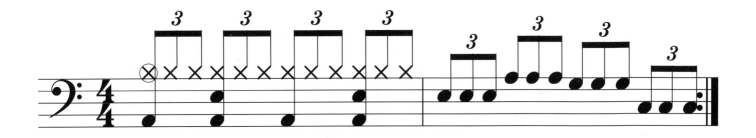

# The Shuffle Rhythm

The shuffle rhythm is created by playing only the first and third notes of the triplet. This is known as **swinging** the notes. The shuffle rhythm is commonly used in many styles of music including Blues, Rock, Country and Jazz. The following example contains one bar of triplets and one bar of the shuffle rhythm. Notice the counting underneath the notes.

 **34.**

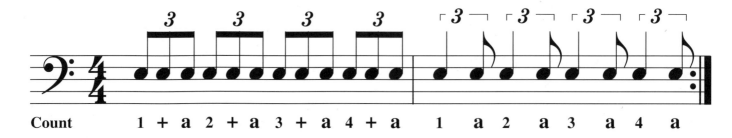

This time the shuffle rhythm is played by the bass drum underneath a triplet right hand part. The snare drum is brought in in the second bar only.

 **35.**

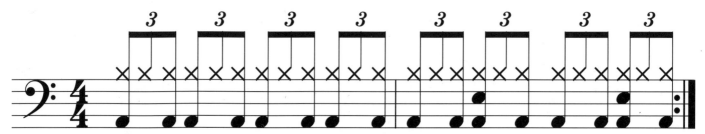

The following examples demonstrate some common shuffle bass drum patterns.

 **36.**

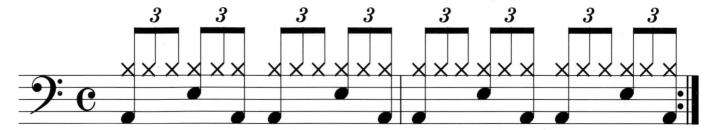

 **37.**

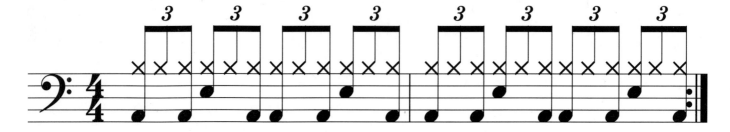

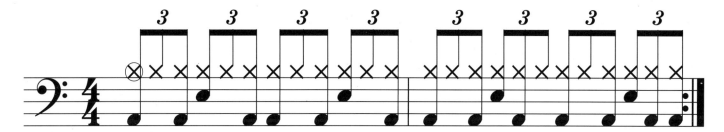

# Notating Swing Rhythms

There are various ways of notating shuffle rhythms and swinging eighth notes. The two outside notes of the triplet group can be grouped together either as a quarter note and an eighth note with a triplet sign above them or as two eighth notes with a rest in between. On the drums these two forms of notation sound exactly the same as demonstrated in the following example.

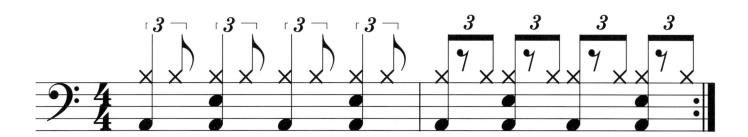

Another common way of indicating that eighth notes are to be swung is to write ♪♪ = ♩♪ at the start of the music and write the whole pattern in eighth notes. Both this and the previous example sound exactly the same, they are just different ways of notating the same rhythm.

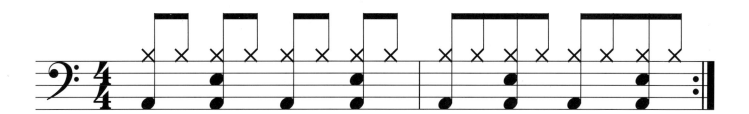

Now you know that eighth notes can be swung, it is important to realise that this makes it possible to play any eighth note groove (beat) with two possible interpretations. The following examples demonstrate a basic beat played first straight and then swung. Go back and try swinging some of the eighth note grooves from earlier in the book.

 ## 40.0 (Played Straight)

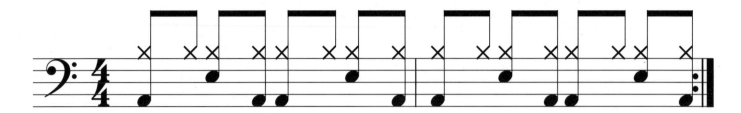

 ## 40.1 (Swung)

Here are two more common shuffle patterns. There are literally thousands of possible drum grooves based on the shuffle rhythm. Experiment with the various techniques you have learned to create some of your own.

 ## 41.

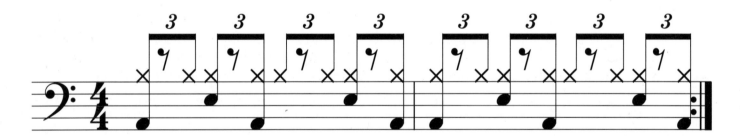

 ## 42.

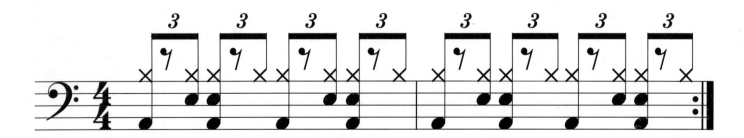

To finish off this lesson, here is another 12 bar Blues solo using a shuffle rhythm. The only real fill here is in the last bar. There is a shorter fill in bar 4 which is incorporated into the groove and a bass drum variation in bar 8 which leads into the crash cymbal on the first beat of the following bar.

 **43.**

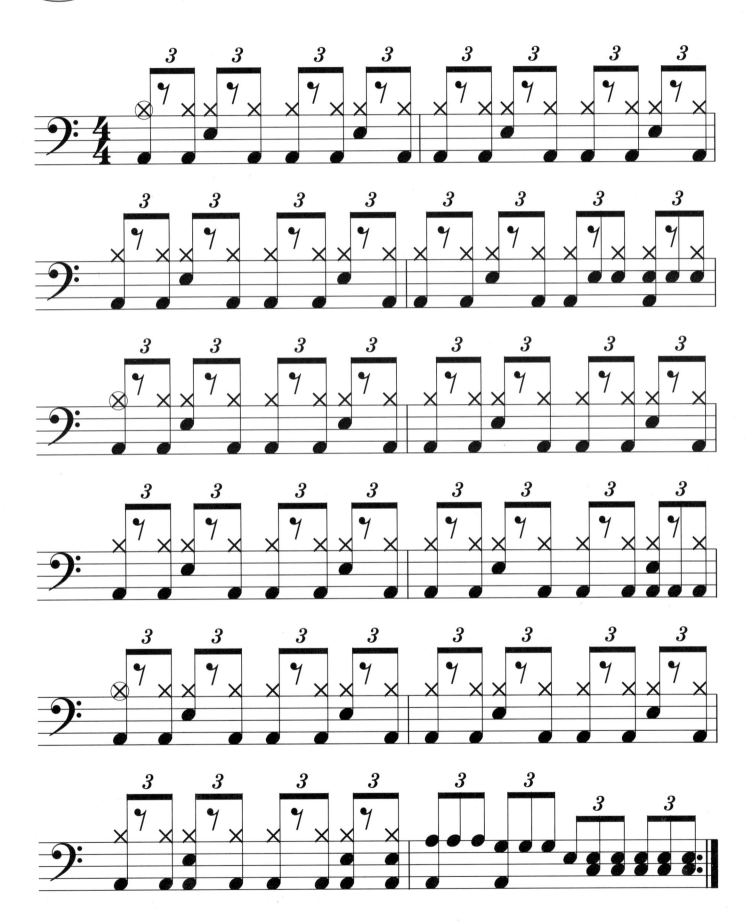

# Lesson 6

## Sixteenth Notes

 This is a **sixteenth note**.
It lasts for **one quarter** of a beat.
There are **four** sixteenth notes in one beat.
There are **16** sixteenth notes in one bar of $\frac{4}{4}$ time.

Two sixteenth notes joined together.

Four sixteenth notes joined together.

Count: 1   e   +   a
Say:   one 'ee' and 'ah'

 **44.0**

The following example contains a bar of sixteenth notes played on the snare drum. Use alternate sticking (**RLRL** and then **LRLR**) and remember to count out loud as you play. Once you have control of the example, try playing it with one hand only (**RRRR** and then **LLLL**). Although this is less common with sixteenth notes, it is used in more advanced drumming and is therefore worth mastering.

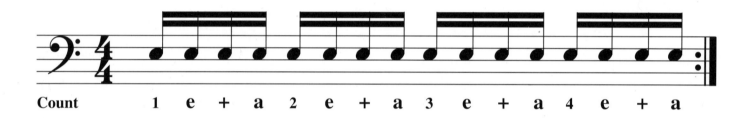

Count        1   e   +   a   2   e   +   a   3   e   +   a   4   e   +   a

 **44.1**

Now try moving between quarter notes, eighth notes and sixteenth notes. Keep the tempo consistent throughout regardless of the type of note being played.

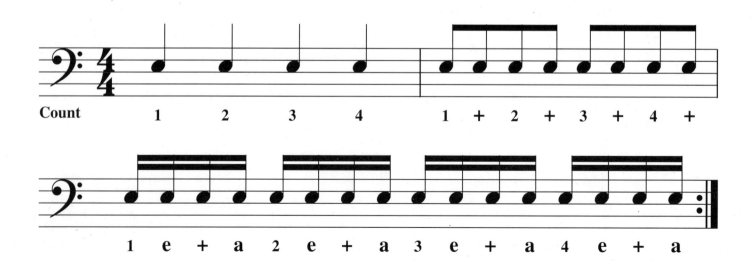

Count        1        2        3        4        1   +   2   +   3   +   4   +

1   e   +   a   2   e   +   a   3   e   +   a   4   e   +   a

Here are two more examples which should help you become familiar with sixteenth notes. Play each one starting with the right hand and then the left hand.

 **44.2**

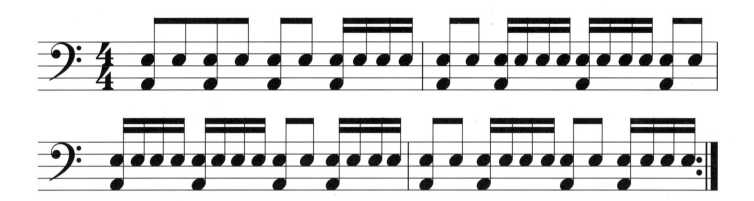

 **44.3**

As well as alternating, this example could also be played using one hand on each particular drum - **RRRR LLLL** etc and **LLLL RRRR** etc.

Now try playing some short fills using sixteenth notes, as demonstrated in the following examples.

**45.0**

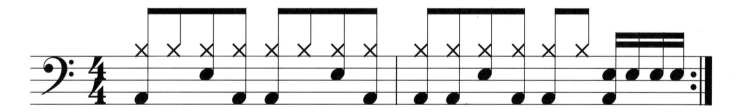

**45.1**

 **46.**

This example makes use of a whole bar sixteenth note fill. Take it slowly at first and practice alternating between the fill and the basic beat.

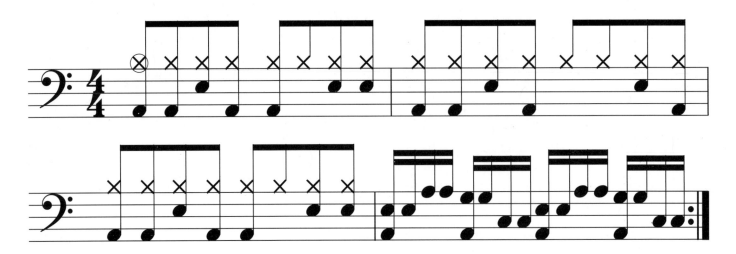

# Two Handed Funk

Here is an example of a common way sixteenth notes are used in Funk. The hi hat is played with alternating right and left hands. In this groove, the right hand plays the backbeat on beats 2 and 4. The hi hat is not played on these beats. If you have trouble with this one, practice the hands only first before adding the bass drum.

 **47. (Hands only)**

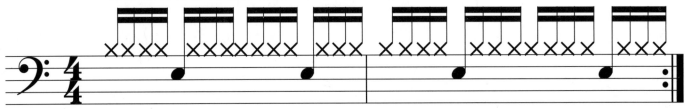

 **48 (Full Groove)**

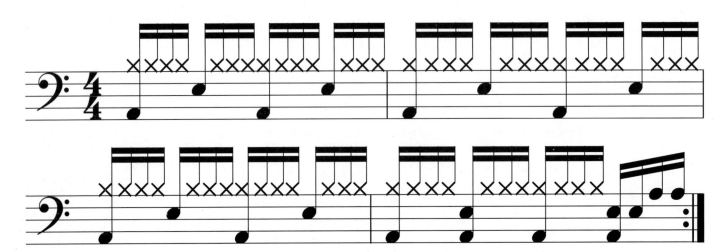

# Sixteenth Note Variations

The following examples demonstrate the use of two common rhythms consisting of two sixteenth notes and an eighth note within a beats. Be sure to count out loud as you play. Play examples 49.0 and 49.1 **RLRL** and **LRLR** as well as **RRRR** and **LLLL**.

 **49.0**

 **49.1**

Once you have control of these rhythms, try playing them on the hi hat with the right hand as demonstrated in the following examples. You could also use these hi hat patterns with some of the eighth note grooves you learned earlier in the book. Experiment!

 **50.**

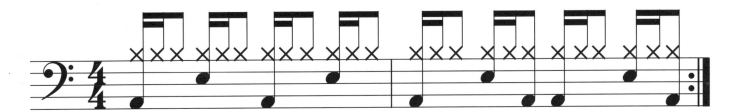

 **51.**

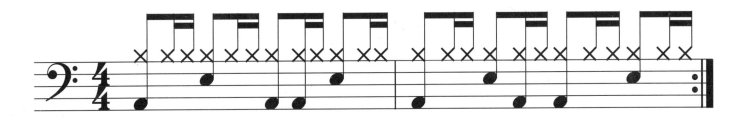

# Lesson 7

## Accents

Sometimes you may want to play certain notes louder than others for dramatic effect. This is when accents are used. An accent is indicated by a wedge mark placed above or below the note as shown below.

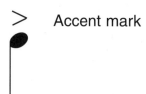

**52.**

This example contains accents both on and off the beat. The accents apply to the snare drum only. When learning accents, the natural tendency is to accent the other limbs as well. However, this is exactly what you need to train yourself **not** to do. Listen carefully to your playing and keep the volume of the bass drum even regardless of whether you are playing an accent on the snare drum or not.

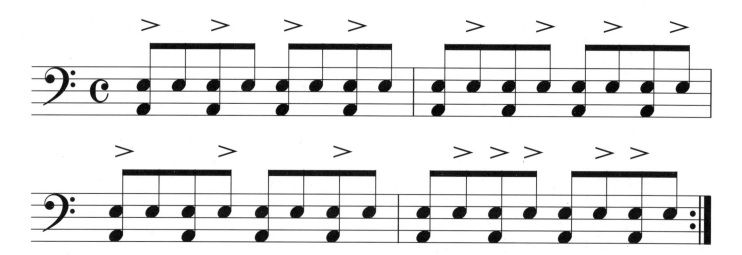

**53.**

Once you are comfortable with the previous example, try this groove which uses accents on the snare drum on the backbeat. Once again, try not to accent the other parts, e.g. the right hand when playing the snare drum accents.

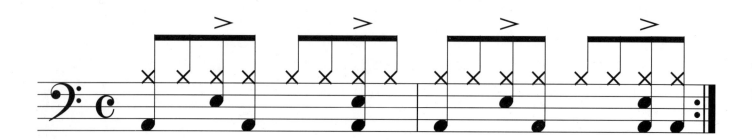

As well as eighth notes, it is important to have control of accents using the other beat subdivisions you have learnt, i.e. triplets and sixteenth notes. Here are some examples to practice. These are only a basic introduction to accents. (For a more in-depth study of accents, see *Progressive Drum Method* by Craig Lauritsen).

 **54.**

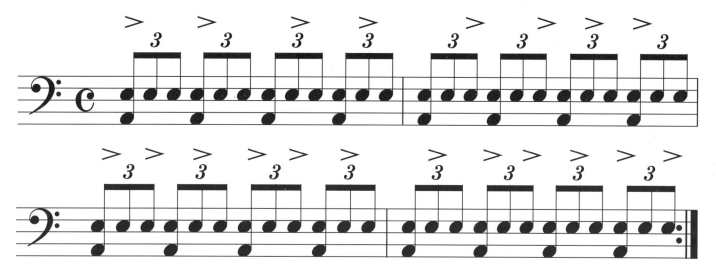

 **55.**

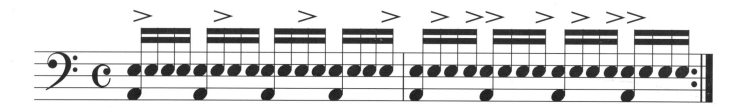

# Accents Using different surfaces

Accents can often be created simply by using different parts of the drumkit. The most common example of this is the use of the crash cymbal. If you play a groove using the hi hat and then play the crash cymbal it automatically gives the effect of an accent even if you don't hit it any harder. Listen to the following example.

 **56.**

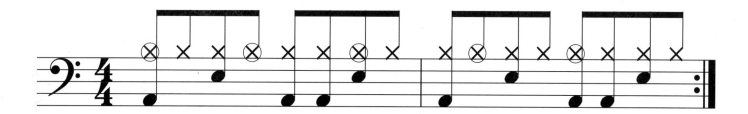

Another common situation where this occurs is in playing a fill. If you play part of a fill on one drum (e.g. snare) and another part of the fill on a different drum (e.g. tom), the difference in tone and the surfaces of the drums will create accents as demonstrated in the following example.

 **57.**

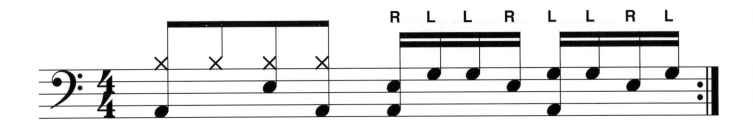

# The Paradiddle

There are particular sticking patterns which lend themselves to playing on different surfaces to create accents. The most common of these patterns is called the **paradiddle**. The basic paradiddle pattern is shown below

# R L R R L R L L

Play this pattern many times until you have is memorised. Try the examples below which apply the paradiddle to different parts of the kit.

 **58.0**

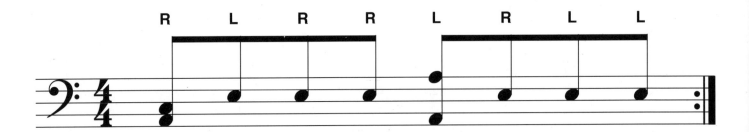

 **58.1**

Once you have mastered the previous example, try using it as a fill as shown here.

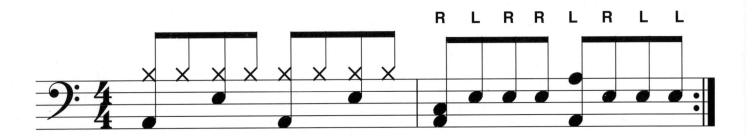

There are many other ways of using the paradiddle between various parts of the drumkit. The paradiddle is an example of a **drum rudiment**. Rudiments are specific sticking patterns which vary the combination of left and right hand movements. The paradiddle is only one of 28 basic rudiments. To become a good drummer, it is worth eventually learning all of the rudiments and applying them to the drumkit. (For a detailed study of rudiments, see *Progressive Drum Method* by Craig Lauritsen).

# Dynamics

The term dynamics refers to the volume at which the music is played. If all music was played at the same volume it would lack expression and would soon become boring. Therefore it is necessary to be able to play at a variety of dynamic levels ranging from very soft to very loud. There are particular markings for dynamics in written music. Some of these are listed below.

| | | | | | |
|---|---|---|---|---|---|
| *pp* | very quiet | *p* | quiet | *mp* | moderately quiet |
| *mf* | moderately loud | *f* | loud | *ff* | very loud |

Two more important symbols used to indicate dynamics are the **crescendo** (meaning a gradual increase in volume) and the **diminuendo** (meaning a gradual decrease in volume). These are shown below.

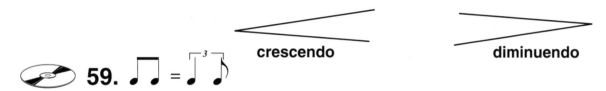

crescendo          diminuendo

**59.**

Observe the dynamic markings in this example and listen to the recording to hear how effective they are when combined with other instruments. Try playing some of the grooves and fills you have learnt at different dynamic levels. The more you practice and play, the easier this becomes. Notice the use of the bar repeat sign in this example.

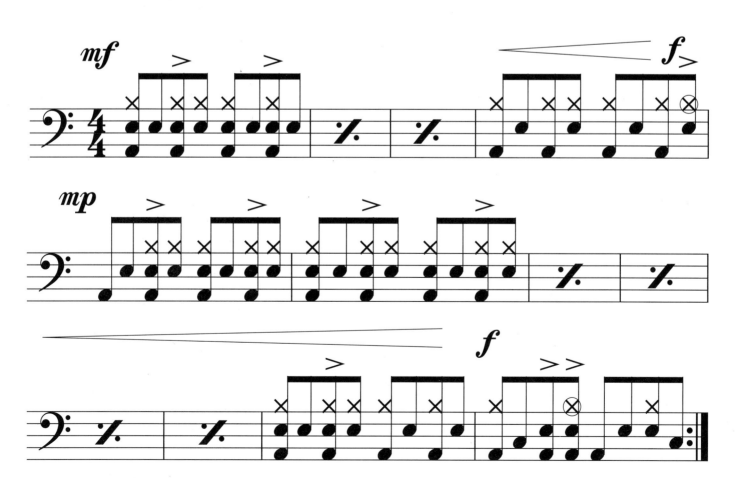

# Dynamic Independence

As mentioned earlier, it is important to be able to play an accent with any one limb without affecting the volume of the other parts. This is called **dynamic independence**. One of the best ways to develop this is to play a basic beat and accent all of the notes played by one of the limbs while keeping the other parts at an even volume. Here are some examples to practice

 **60.0  (Snare Drum)**

 **60.1  (Bass Drum)**

 **60.2  (Hi Hat)**

 **60.3  (Bass Drum and Backbeat))**

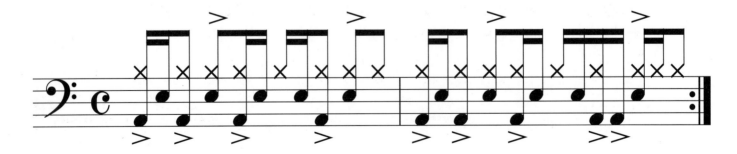

# Ghost Notes

Another important aspect of dynamics is the use of ghost notes. Whereas an accent is a note played louder than the other notes being played, a ghost note is played softer than most other notes and is the reverse of an accent. Ghost notes are common in more advanced drumming, particularly in Funk and Jazz. Ghost notes are often indicated by a bracket around the note, as shown below.

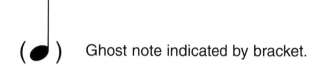

Ghost note indicated by bracket.

Ghost notes are most commonly played on the snare drum. Play the following example and listen carefully to the volume of your notes.

 **61.**

Once you have control of ghost notes on the snare, try the following Funk beats which contain ghost notes. If you have trouble playing them, practice each one two limbs at a time and count as you play.

 **62.**

 **63.**

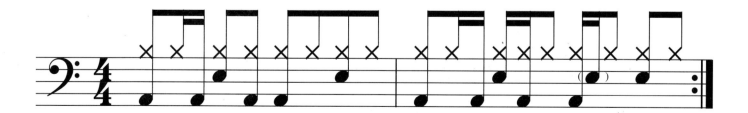

 **64.**

This one is a shuffle groove which is commonly used in Blues. It is often called a **Chicago shuffle** or **double shuffle**.

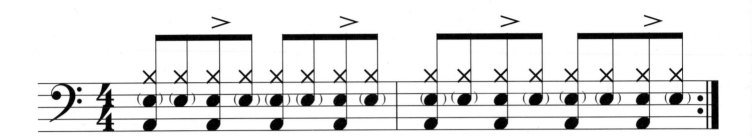

 **65.**

**66.**

This one has a fill in the fourth bar which makes use of the paradiddle. These last two beats may take some time to play well, but stick with it and your practice will definitely pay off.

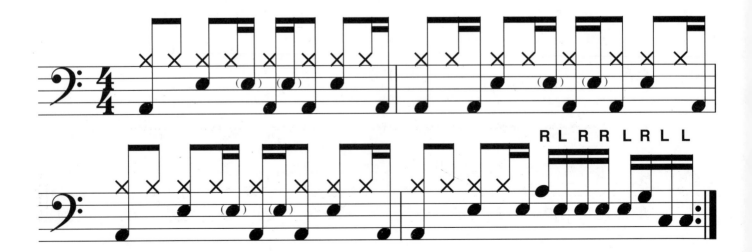

# Lesson 8

## Using the Left Foot

Up to this point the beats have used only three limbs but as mentioned before, good drummers have control over all four limbs. The left foot is most commonly used to control the opening and closing of the hi hat cymbals. The hi hat played with the foot is notated in the same position on the staff as the bass drum, except that an X symbol is used instead of a notehead. Practice the example below which uses only the left foot. As with previous examples, keep a steady tempo and aim for a consistent sound and volume.

 **67.**

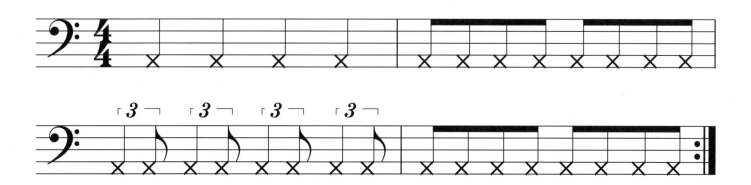

Once you are comfortable with the previous example, play a drum beat using the left foot on the backbeat instead of the left hand. Since you are opening and closing the hi-hat with the left foot, play the right hand part on the ride cymbal instead. Here are some examples.

 **68.0**

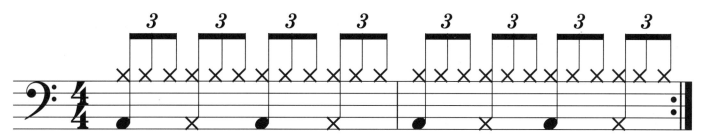

 **68.1**

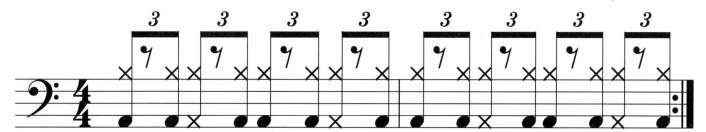

# Jazz Beats

The following example demonstrates the most basic form of the Jazz or Swing beat. Once again the right hand plays the ride cymbal while the left foot plays the hi hat on the backbeat.

 **69.**

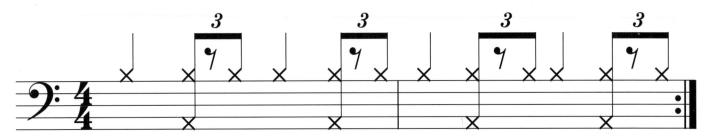

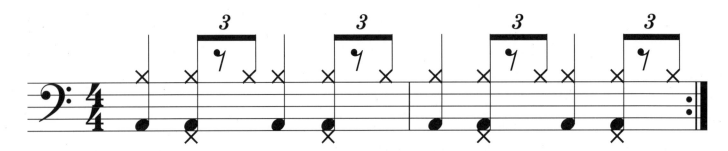 **70.**

Here is the same beat with the bass drum added. When both feet play together, the hi hat symbol appears under the bass drum note in the written music.

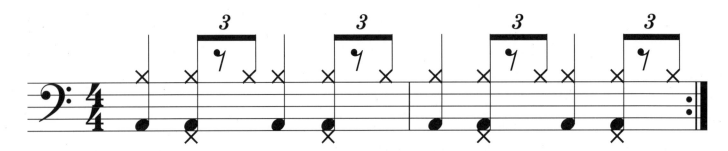

# Side Stick

Because the hi hat played with the foot is a fairly quiet sound, a technique known as side stick or cross stick is sometimes used on the snare drum when the left foot is playing the hi hat. With this technique, the stick is played against the rim of the snare drum as shown in the photo below. Place the heel of your hand in the centre of the snare drum, with the butt of the stick protruding over the counter hoop by approximately three inches (8 centimetres).

**71.**

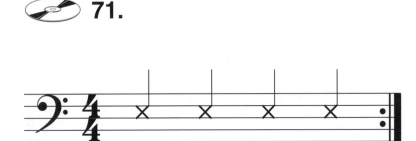

Try using the side stick technique with the following examples which are Jazz beat variations.

**72.0**

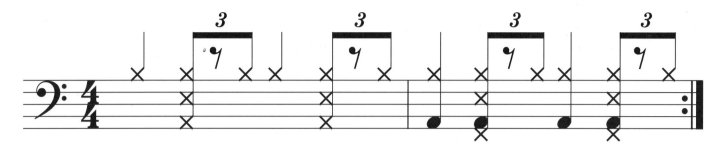

**72.1**

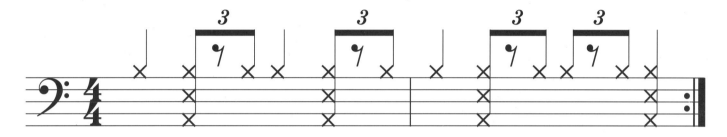

**72.2**

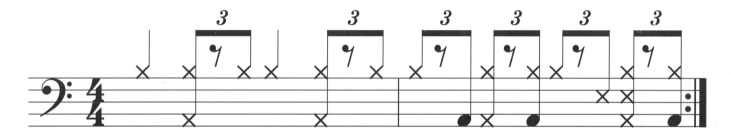

# Playing the Open Hi-Hat

Another important drum technique involves releasing the pressure of the left foot to partially open the hi hat cymbals and then playing the open hi hat with the side of the stick. An open hi hat is notated by a small **o** above the note. The hi hat is then closed where an **X** appears and played as normal until the next **o** symbol appears. Listen to the following example on the CD to hear the effect this produces. The exact degree of opening is up to you. Experiment until you are happy with the sound, but don't open it too far or the sound becomes sloppy and makes it difficult to keep good time.

**73.0**

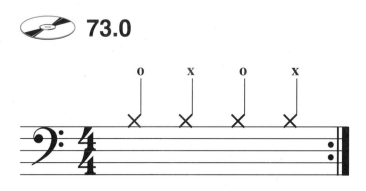

## 73.1

In this example the open hi hat is played on the second and fourth beats of the bar. Practice the technique until you are comfortable playing either open or closed hi hat on any beat of the bar.

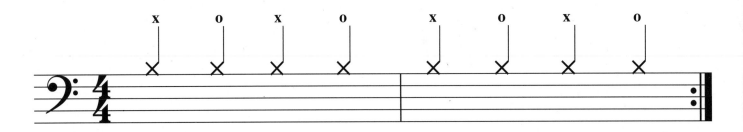

## 74.

The next step is to add the bass drum and snare drum. Practice this example many times until you are totally comfortable with it.

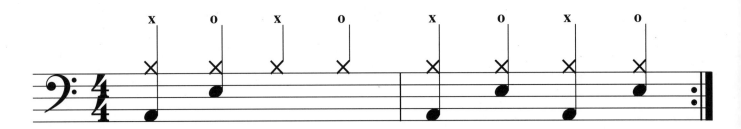

## 75.

Once you can play the previous example, try this groove which uses eighth notes on the hi hat, which is opened on the "**and**" section of each beat.

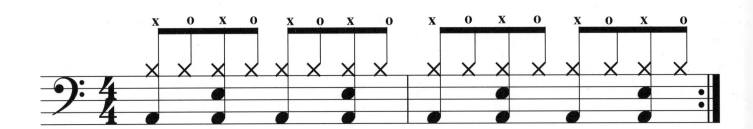

Here are some more grooves which make use of the open hi hat technique. Take them slowly at first if necessary and as always, remember to count out loud as you play.

## 76.

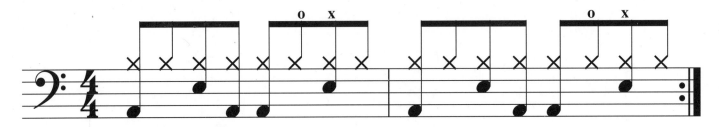

**77.**

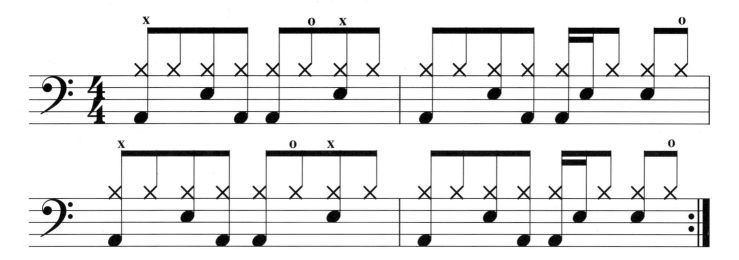

**78.**

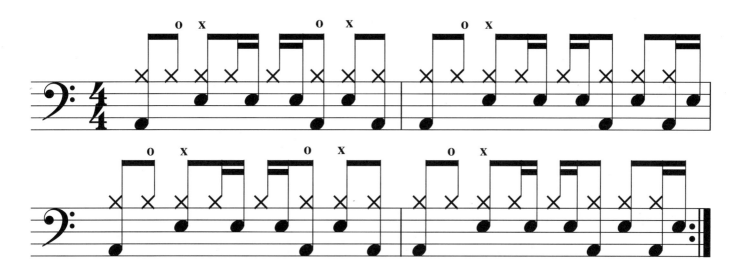

Here is a typical Swing example making use of the open hi hat technique. Remember not to open the hi hats too much, just enough to get the desired sound.

**79.**

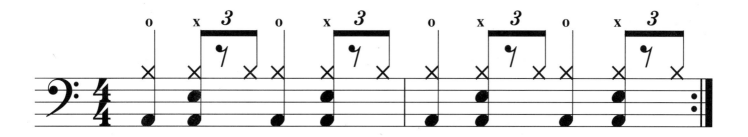

# Lesson 9

## The Three Four Time Signature ( $\frac{3}{4}$ )

 This time signature is called the **three four** time signature. It tells you there are **three** beats in each bar. Three four time is also known as waltz time. There are **three** quarter notes in one bar of time.

Up to this point, everything you have learnt has been in $\frac{4}{4}$ time. Most songs you play will be in $\frac{4}{4}$ time, but occasionally you will encounter other key signatures. Three four time ( $\frac{3}{4}$ ) is also based on quarter notes, but there are three beats per bar instead of four. A good way to get started with $\frac{3}{4}$ time is to play the bass drum on the first beat of the bar and the hi hat with the left foot on beats two and three as demonstrated in the following example.

 **80.0**

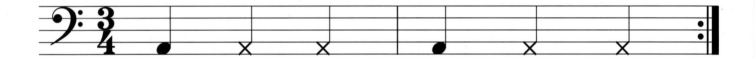

 **80.1**

Next, try adding the ride cymbal and the snare drum. Remember to count as you play.

**81.**

A basic Swing beat in $\frac{3}{4}$ time can be created by playing swing eighth notes on the second beat.

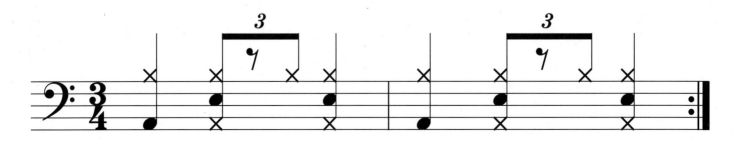

**82.**

Here is a slightly more complex two bar pattern. Experiment and make up some of your own beats.

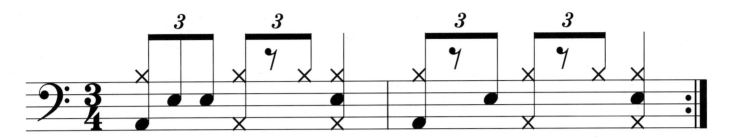

**83.**

Don't forget to try out some ¾ beats using straight eighth notes as well as swing eighth notes.

# The Twelve Eight Time Signature (12/8)

This time signature is called the **twelve eight** time signature. It tells you there are **twelve eighth note beats** in each bar.

A bar of eighth notes in twelve eight time sounds the same as a bar of triplets in four four time. Although there are twelve individual beats which can be counted, twelve eight time is usually still counted in four as demonstrated in the following example.

**84.**

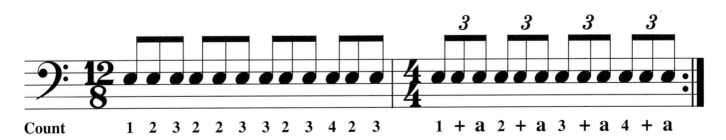

Count     1 2 3 2 2 3 3 2 3 4 2 3     1 + a 2 + a 3 + a 4 + a

Here are some typical beats in twelve eight time.

 **85.**

 **86.**

 **87.**

One of the main reasons for using the twelve eight time signature instead of $\frac{4}{4}$ is that it becomes easier to count when the eighth notes are subdivided. Since there is a number on each eighth note, sixteenth notes can be counted as **+** (**and**) as demonstrated in the following example.

 **88.**

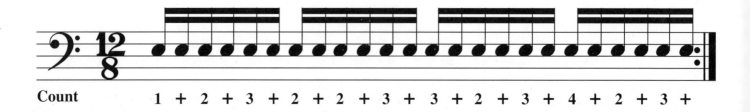

Count      1 + 2 + 3 + 2 + 2 + 3 + 3 + 2 + 3 + 4 + 2 + 3 +

**89.0**

The right hand part in this example shows one of the common ways sixteenth notes are used in twelve eight time.

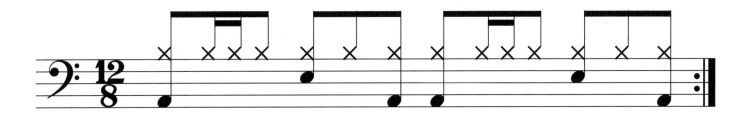

 **89.1 (swing 16ths)**

This example is notated exactly the same as the previous one, but on the recording the sixteenth notes are swung. Listen to the CD to hear the difference. Swinging sixteenth notes is common in twelve eight time.

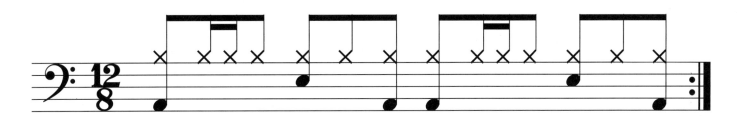

 **90.**

Here is another twelve eight groove which makes use of swinging sixteenth notes. In the last part of the fill in bar 2, the left hand plays the snare while the right hand plays the floor tom.

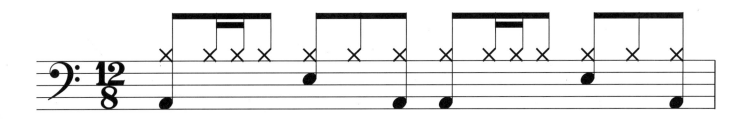

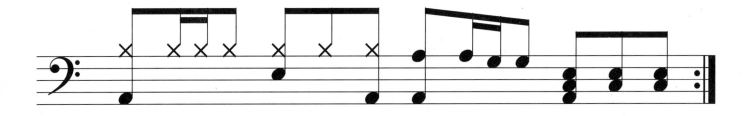

# Twelve Eight Time Solo

To finish off this lesson, here is a 12 bar Blues solo in twelve eight time. Listen to the CD to hear how the drum part locks in with the bass and the guitar. This is very important when playing with a band, which is the subject of lesson 10. On the recording of this example, the right hand switches to the ride cymbal and the whole drum part contains several variations, see if you can work them out by ear. This is an important skill to develop. Start working out the drum parts from some of your favorite albums.

 **91.**

# Lesson 10

## Playing With a Band

Learning to fit your part with other instruments is very important for a drummer. While a guitarist or piano player can play solo, the drums are really made for playing with a band. When you are playing with other musicians, the most important thing is to listen to each other and try to respond to what the other players are doing. In an ideal band, everyone is equally responsible for keeping good time but in reality, many musicians (especially guitarists who play by ear only) neglect the study of rhythm and beat subdivisions and rely on the drummer to keep good time and indicate what is happening rhythmically. While a singer or horn player has time to breathe between phrases and a guitarist or keyboard player leaves space between lines or chords, the drummer and bass player have to play consistently to keep the groove going and feeling good. When practicing drum parts for songs, play the basic groove over and over until you can do it easily in a relaxed manner and you feel good playing it. Then try adding a few fills and variations. If you are not comfortable doing a particular part, leave it out (when in doubt, leave it out) until you have practiced it some more by yourself with a drum machine or metronome. **The bottom line is that the time should always be strong and solid and the groove should feel good**.

When you play a song for the first time, start with a simple beat and listen to what the other musicians are doing. Then try modifying your part to fit in with and complement their parts.Of all the other instruments in the band, the **bass** is the one you will need to work closest with. The following example demonstrates a basic Rock beat with a constant eighth note bass line. Listen to the CD to hear how they sound together.

**92.0**

**Bass**

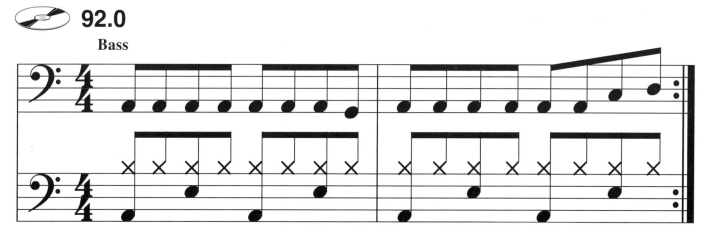

If you wanted to change the drum part to make it sound more interesting and fit better with the bass line, there are a couple of things you could look for in the bass line itself. Notice that the bass plays a lower note at the end of the first bar, before returning to the original note. This variation would be a good place to add another bass drum note. Also notice the higher variation in the end of bar 2. Here you could also add a higher sound such as an open hi hat. Listen to the CD to hear the effect this creates. A great way to practice these things is to **sing the bass line** while you play your drum part.

**92.1**

**Bass**

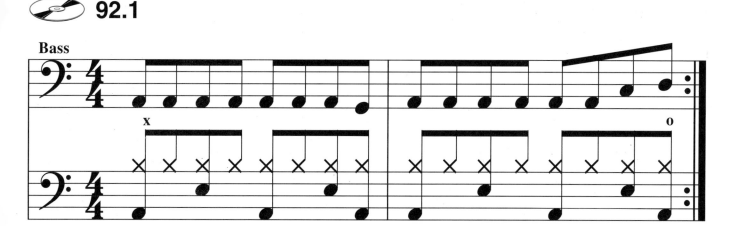

# Working With a Guitar

When you are jamming with a band, any member of the band could come up with the first part that the others then fit in with. Just say the guitarist comes up with a rhythm part like the one in the following example.

 **93.0**

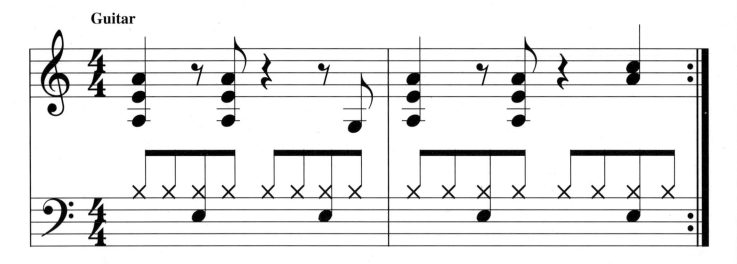

Once again, there are several things you could do to create a drum part that fits well with the guitar part. The snare backbeat already works well because it falls in the spaces between the guitar notes and creates interplay between the parts. Another thing you could add is a bass drum part which coincides with the guitar part on the "and" section of the second beat. You could also play an extra snare drum hit to coincide with the guitar part. As with the previous bass example you could add a bass drum note to fit in with the low guitar note at the end of bar 1. Listen to the CD a few times to hear how these things work.

 **93.1**

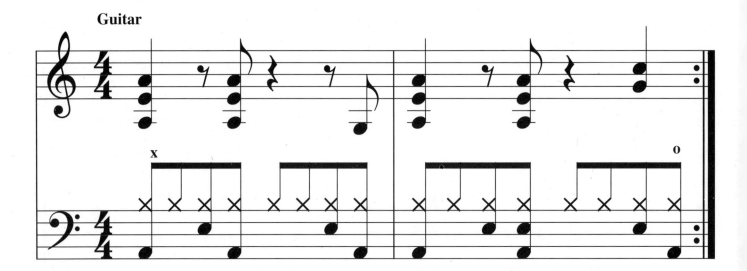

 **94.**

Now listen to how these parts work with the bass line from earlier in the lesson. All the parts lock in to create a solid groove which would be great for someone to sing with or play a lead solo with.

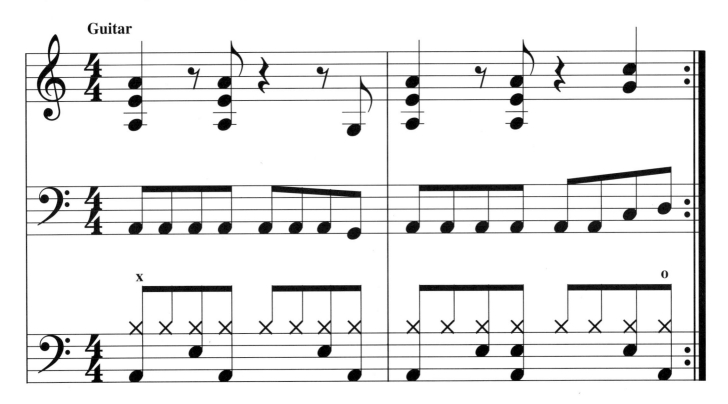

 **95.**

Another thing that works well in a band situation is for the drummer to play a fill along with a lead guitar. This kind of thing usually needs to be rehearsed well at first, but once you get to know how each other plays, you can improvise fills together. Once again listen to the CD to hear how effective this sounds.

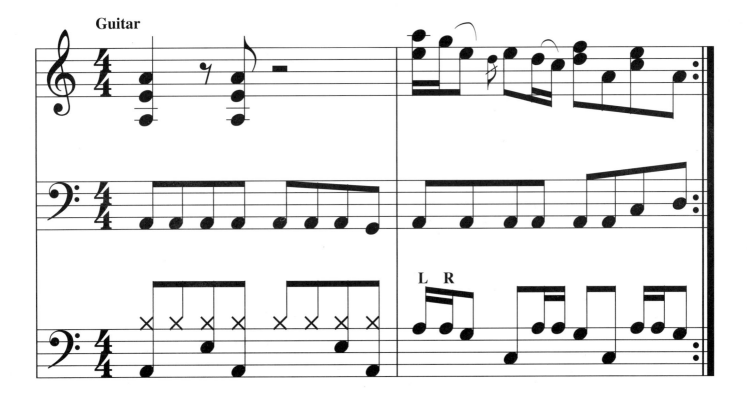

 **96.**

Fills add variety and excitement but can also ruin a song if over used or played in the wrong place. The fill shown here sounds great at the end of the section and leads back to the main groove. However, if you played this fill all the way through, it would destroy any vocal line sung over it and would sound too busy and cluttered. Once again, **listening** and thinking about how best to serve the song is the most important thing when deciding when to add fills. This applies equally to all instruments.

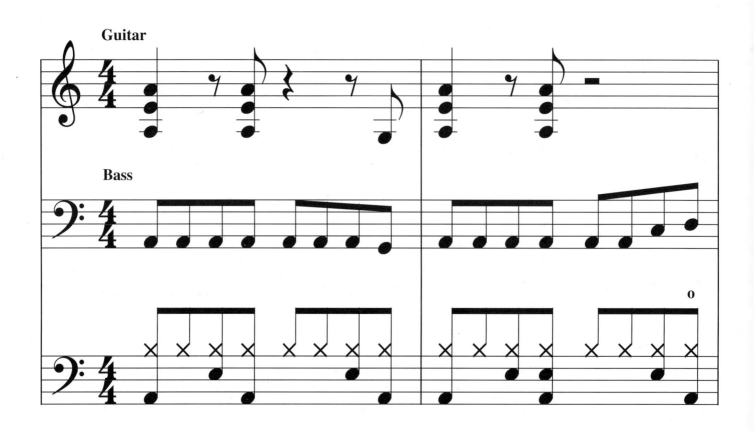

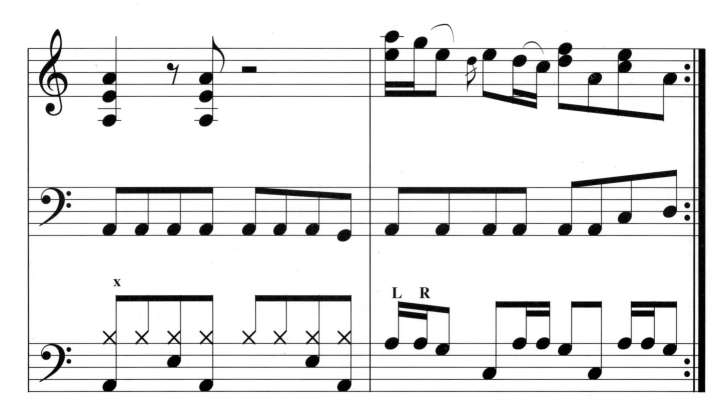

# Musical Form

The term "musical form" refers to the structure of a song or piece of music, e.g. verse, verse, chorus, verse, or 12 bar Blues. Most songs you play in a band situation fall into two categories. One is the 12 bar Blues form which you have already learnt and the other is songs which break down into 8 or 16 bar sections. When you are playing a song, it is important to think about the length of sections or verses as this largely determines the way all of the musicians will play. Listen to some of your favourite songs and notice the way the drum part changes, e.g. fills, crash cymbal etc at the end and beginning of verses. Listen also to dynamics and interplay between the parts. A great way to practice getting control of the form of a song is to sing the lyrics as you play your part. In fact, singing is great for your coordination and independance as well as making you much more aware of what your drum part is ultimately fitting in with and complementing. Another useful exercise is to actually count the bar numbers as you play. E.g if you are playing a song in $\frac{4}{4}$ time, instead of counting 1 2 3 4, 1 2 3 4, you could count **1 2 3 4, 2 2 3 4, 3 2 3 4, 4 2 3 4** etc. After a while you begin to know instinctively where you are in the song. Written below are typical examples of an 8 bar form and a 12 bar Blues form. Each one has chord symbols written above it just as you would find on a song chart. Chords are discussed on page 60.

# 8 Bar Form

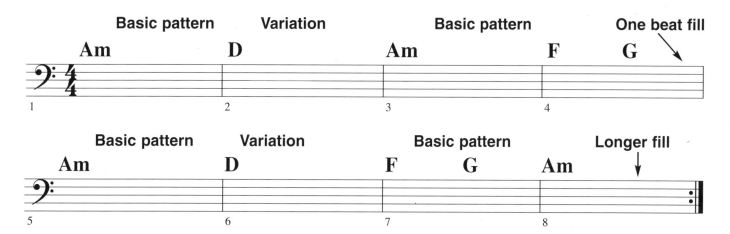

# 12 Bar Blues

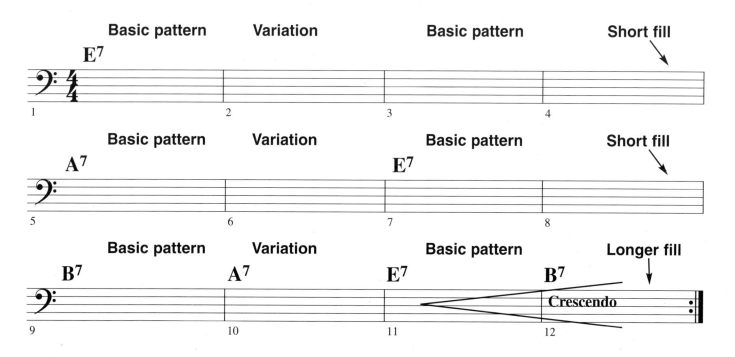

# Understanding Music

By now you should have a good basic understanding of how rhythm works, how beats cand be subdivided and how dynamics work. However, just as many instrumentalists neglect their rhythm skills, many drummers also neglect developing an understanding of the other aspects of music such as melody, (e.g vocals or lead guitar) and harmony e.g (keyboard or rhythms guitar). If you have a basic understanding of these subjects you can contribute much more to band arrangements and songwriting. In fact, it is strongly recommended that you learn at least a bit of general music by taking up bass, guitar or keyboards. Ask the other musicians you play with about what they are doing and get them to show you a few things. Of course, the drums will still be your main instrument, but drummers who understand music are always popular and usually get lots of work. Lets look at the musical tools used to create melody and harmony.

## Music Notes

There are only seven letters used for notes in music. They are:

**A   B   C   D   E   F   G**

These notes are known as the **musical alphabet.**

## Melody and Scales

Most melodies are derived from **scales**. A scale is a pattern of notes at different pitches, which can be repeated in higher or lower registers and played on any melodic instruments. Most bass lines and lead solos are made up of notes from scales. A scale may start on any pitch and the name of the starting note of the scale determines the name of the scale. The most common building block for melody is the **major scale**. The simplest of these is the **C major scale**, which starts and ends on the note C and contains all of the natural notes used in music.

A **major scale** is a group of eight notes that produces the familiar sound:

**Do   Re   Mi   Fa   So   La   Ti   Do**

**C    D    E    F    G    A    B    C**

The following example demonstrates the C major scale played by the bass and the guitar. Don't worry if you can't read the notes, just notice that there is a different pitched dot for each note.

**97.0**

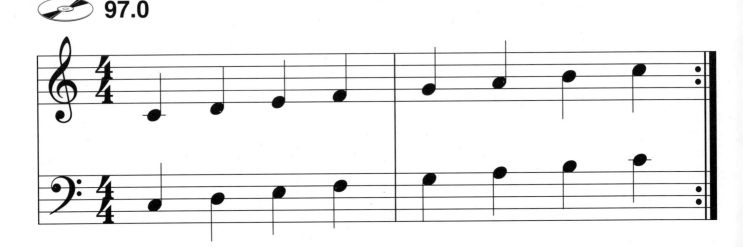

You may have noticed that the notes were in different places on the staff for the bass and the guitar. The bass uses the bass staff, which is the same staff used for drum music but the guitar uses the treble clef and treble staff which are shown below. Melodic instruments may use either the bass staff or the treble staff. Keyboard music usually uses both.

## The Treble Clef

This symbol is called a **treble clef**. There is a treble clef at the beginning of every line of guitar music.

## The Treble Staff

A staff with a treble clef written on it is called a **treble staff**.

In the following example, all of the notes played by the guitar and the bass come from the C major scale. Just as drummers make use of various note values to create beats and fills, instrumentalists can combine the notes from a scale in endless ways to create melodies such as bass lines and lead solos.

**97.1**

See how music can be created from this simple group of notes. The major scale is only one of many types of scales. To find out more about scales and how they work, see *Progressive Music Theory*, as well as asking the musicians you play with and experimenting on an instrument capable of playing melodies. There is obviously a lot more to music theory than the information in this lesson. To make you a more confident and well rounded musician, it is really worth your while to learn all you can about the way music is put together and the language used to explain it.

# Harmony and Chords

Harmony can be thought of as the notes that support and add character to a melody. The basic building blocks of harmony are chords. A chord is a group of notes played simultaneously (e.g. strumming on a guitar. There are many different types of chords which have different names and sounds. If you look at sheet music you will see chord symbols written above the melody. These symbols will be things like C, Cm, Bb7, E7♯9 etc. All these symbols describe chords which have different types of sounds. Chords are usually played in a repeating sequence called a **chord progression**. A chord progression works a bit like a basic drum beat, except that the sequence may repeat every 2, 4, 8, or 12 bars instead of every one or two bars. Once again, the best way to learn about chords is to learn a bit of basic guitar or keyboard. In the final examples written below, the guitar plays a chord progression and the bass plays a melody (bassline). All the parts combine to give a strong sense of rhythm. Put these parts together and you have the three basic elements of music, **rhythm**, **melody** and **harmony**.

**98.**

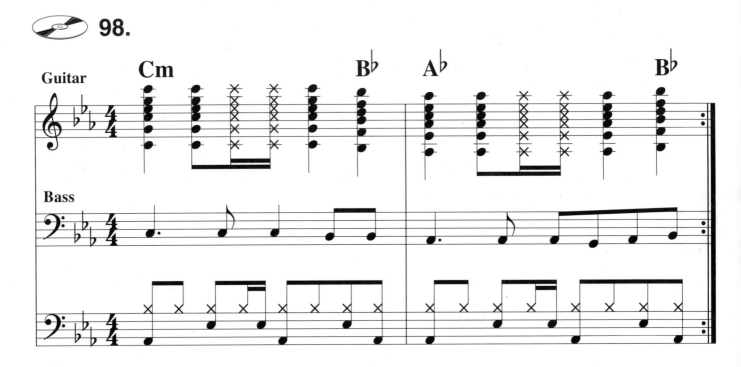

**99.**

(Play 4 times)